HEART OF THE GAME

To all of the people around the world who have supported minor hockey as parents, coaches, officials, sponsors and volunteers. Every year, with your help, thousands of tiny boys and girls take their first unsteady steps onto the ice and in time they play their first "Hockey Game" – the greatest game in the world.

Heart of the Game
Copyright 2002 John Newby

National Library of Canada CIP data available
ISBN 1-55366-326-8

Winding Stair Press
An imprint of Stewart House Publishing Inc.
290 North Queen Street, # 210
Etobicoke, Ontario, M9C 5K4
Canada
1-866-574-6873
www.stewarthousepub.com

Executive V.P. and Publisher: Ken Proctor
Director of Publishing and Acquisitions, Young Readers: Susan Jasper
Cover and Interior design: Counterpunch/Peter Ross
Editor: Susan Menchinton

This book is available at special discounts for bulk purchases by groups or organizations for sales promotions, premiums, fundraising and educational purposes. For details, contact: Peter March, Stewart House Publishing Inc., Special Sales Department, 195 Allstate Parkway, Markham, Ontario, L3R 4T8 Toll Free 1-866-474-3478

Printed and bound in Canada

John Newby's artwork is available for purchase on www.john-newby.com or from John Newby Art Gallery
108 Queen St
Niagara-on-the-lake, Ontario, L0S 1J0
Canada
905-468-0032
charisma@ont.net

Heart of the Game

MINOR HOCKEY MOMENTS

John Newby

WINDING
STAIR
PRESS

Early practice, 5 a.m.

you're already awake when the alarm goes off.

Pull on your gear,

strap on the shin guards, adjust the helmet –

you're ready to go,

you're part of a team.

You imagine being the best there is.

Game time's coming,

there's so much to think about –

so much to absorb.

Dreaming of victory –

of playing at the highest level.

This sweater's too big?

But in your mind you're already there.

Outside, playing shinny with windblown faces.

Frozen fingers and toes won't matter –

you'll quit when you can't see the puck.

As a rookie, falling is your best skill,

but chasing the puck, doing drills,

you learn what a rebound is

and what to do with a drop pass.

13

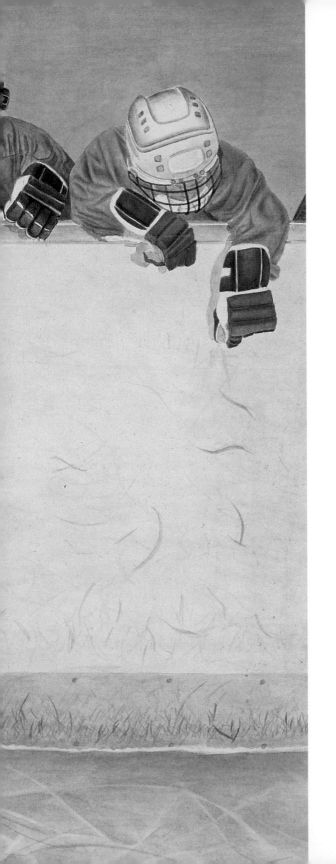

Sometimes it's hard just to keep your gear on.

Coach can fix anything,

he makes the games fun for you –

he remembers what it's like to be a kid.

Your first trip to the penalty box –

you didn't mean for the other guy to fall.

"Two for roughing,"

What's that?

You learn the skills, slowly.

Skating, shooting, passing,

working the corners, digging out the puck.

The wraparound, a goal-mouth scramble, going upstairs –

good things happen when you go to the net.

And more than just skills

you learn respect –

for your team, for the coach,

for the rules, for the officials.

It's not going to be easy.

You won't always be right

but you learn from mistakes.

It all comes down to team play.

You follow the action and wait for your shift.

Forwards on a breakaway!

You want to get out there.

It's your turn now.

Deke around the defenseman –

this goalie's blocked every shot.

You flub it,

but the puck trickles in anyway!

Not pretty, but it counts.

Can you handle the call when you don't think its fair?

Just keep it cool –

kill off the penalty and get back in the game.

A high, hard shot beats the goalie.

The center celebrates,

teammates cheer.

The goalie gets the puck

and the defenseman slumps.

This is just a moment in time –

there's another game tomorrow.

So the years will pass,

and playing hockey

will be a part of who you are.

You'll want to share what you've learned –

patience, discipline, teamwork, respect,

your love for this sport...

found at the heart of the game.

Glossary of Hockey Terms and Phrases

assist credit given to a player who passes the puck to a teammate who then scores

block to prevent a shot on goal

blue line one of two blue lines that divide the ice into three zones

boards wooden structure around the playing surface

center one of three forward positions and the player who usually takes face-offs

center line a red line which divides the rink in half

chasing the puck skating after a loose puck

coach person who teaches and trains the team

defenseman a player who tries to stop the other team from getting a shot on goal

deke to pretend to move the puck to make the opposing player move out of position

digging out the puck to get the puck away from another player who is holding it against the boards

drills activities practiced by a team to help teach them basic hockey skills

drop pass when a player leaves the puck behind him for a teammate who is following

face-off dropping of the puck to start up play

forward one of three players on the ice; center, left winger, right winger, whose job it is to score

game time the time a game is scheduled to begin

gear special clothing and equipment worn by a player

goal when the puck crosses the goal line into the net; teams get one point for each goal

goal-mouth scramble when many players are fighting for the puck in front of the net

goalie the player on each team who protects the net area and stops the other team from scoring

going upstairs to shoot the puck toward the top of the net

helmet protective headgear worn by each player

net woven mesh on a metal frame; the area the goalie protects from goals

officials includes referees, who skate with the players during a game to see if any rules are broken

on a breakaway a scoring chance where there are no defenseman between the puck carrier and the goalie

passing moving the puck from player to player

penalty punishment for breaking the rules, making a player leave the ice for a length of time

penalty box a small bench near the score keeper where players are sent to serve their penalties

power-play when one team has more players on the ice because the other team has taken a penalty

practice to repeat an activity over and over to improve a skill

puck a hard, black rubber disk used to score goals in hockey

rebound when the puck springs back into play after a goalie makes a save

rookie a beginning player

rules a list of what players can and can't do when playing a game

save when a goalie blocks the puck from going in the net

shift a player's turn on the ice

shin guards protective pads worn on the legs by all players

shinny a loose game of hockey with few players and little equipment – also called a pick-up game

shooting sending the puck down the ice with force and speed

shot when a player shoots the puck at the net

skating to glide on or move along the ice on skates

skill ability gained by practicing

sweater a hockey jersey worn on the upper body

teammates all the players on one team

trip to knock a player over with your stick or foot – if caught this causes a penalty to be called

two for roughing a two-minute penalty awarded when a player pushes or is too rough.

victory winning the game or series

winger a player who is one of two forward positions; right or left wing

working the corners trying to move the puck along the boards near the opposing net

wraparound to come from behind the net and slide the puck in before the goalie sees you